"Purple is such a twisted, complex color-it conveys the passion of red, the sadness of blue, the depravity of black. Purple is neither happy nor sad. It is pain and despair but longing, too- fiery desire, beaten and bruised but struggling onward, determined to overcome, to move forward rather than retreat." -James Paterson, Invisible

Purple.

For Lauren Janelle

All my life I've had to fight.

10   Sista, You Been on my Mind

15   You Shole is Ugly

17   Till You do Right by Me

19   Who this Woman?

20   A Little Shug Avery Pee

22   Think about Heaven Later

24   Fine With Me

26   I Think it Pisses God Off

28   When the Last Time Somebody Comb her Hair

29   And you Can Stay all Day

30   You're a Woman. You're Nothing at All.

32   Never Asked you for Anything.

34   It's Going to Rain on Your Head

35   Get My Children out of Here

36   Speak Lord

I never meant to cause you any sorrow.

40 Baby I'm a Star

42 The Beautiful Ones

44 Insatiable

46 Let's Go Crazy!

47 Take Me with You

48 Adore

49 The Glamourous Life

50 Round and Round

52 Kiss

53 Still Waiting

55 A Love Bizarre

56 Sexy Mutha@#$%!*

57 One Song

59 If I Was Your Girlfriend

All my life I've had to fight.

Sista, You Been On my Mind

It goes against my religion

to suffer or celebrate in solitude

That, to me, is an alternative lifestyle in which I do not believe

I believe in God and

I believe in sisters

A sister will

interrupt your rant to pray for you

insist the world still needs you

when it feels like no one will notice if you are not here

will remind you of your brilliance

and call you on your b.s.

Way after my parents stopped collaborating on love projects

the Creator continued to send me more sisters

born of other mothers

but connected to me

Those connections

served as cushion

for a transitional season

We may not all share blood

but we will draw blood

for each other

To the ones who know my secrets

To the ones who listened without judgment

but injected some realness to my fairytale-d perspective

To the one that never called me stupid

Or said I told you so

This is for you

To the one who forced me to buy a test

and take the test and then held me until I stopped crying

To the first person to say congratulations

To the one who fielded answers to questions that were nobody's business

To the one who helped me break the news to my father

To the one who made me look forward

sat next to me in the classes

to the one who tied my shoe when I couldn't see it or reach it

to the ones who showered me with love

This is for you

To the ones who told me I could be good at this, I would be good at
this

to the ones who massaged my massive belly and willed the already
stubborn life inside to switch directions so he could come out the right way

he came out right

to the ones who gathered round my bed waiting

to the one who held my left leg as I pushed my way into a new beginning

to the one who taught me not to trip when things ain't perfect

and then told me how to do the paperwork

and asked me repeatedly when I was going to take care of the paperwork

to the one who saw me and gave me a
wordless hug in family court

to the other one who saw me and gave me
a wordless hug in family court

to the one who reminds me to keep it classy
in these streets when I
want to be ugly

to the one who said "we may run into him
tonight and b!tch you betta
not cry"

to the ones who offer solutions that involve
ninja suits, getaway cars
and bail money

to the ones who make it so I do not miss
work or my turn on the mic

or a chance to paint my nails or take a nap

to the ones my son prefers when he tires of
me

This is for you

To the ones who expect to get what they
give

and for the ones who don't

I would be less than good if God had not
sent you

thank you seems insufficient

But I thank you

you and me, us neva part

single mothering is not for the faint of heart

or for anyone who has the unfortunate task

of navigating this life without sisters

You Shole is Ugly

I had been fast and
loose with the sun in high school

Allowing it to
have its way with me any time it wanted to

Warnings from
the cutest guy in class about getting too
black

Didn't prevent
him from doubling back to catch extra
glimpses of my ebony

When I cut off all my hair I was warned
I might get invisible to men
But the funny thing is
the exact opposite happened

and the food was so good down at Morgan
State
I added on a whole heap of weight
well apparently it all went to the right places
because
them men sho enuf came runnin

and then I lost most of it

and "only a dog likes bones"
well somebody should have told that to my phone
because it never did stop ringing

and then I was no longer so young
"these cats ain't checkin for nobody over twenty one"

grown up woman can't get no fun
but I stays with an invitation to party

then I had me a baby
and everybody knows
"nobody wants somebody else's baby mama"
except, that ain't a little bit true

I always knew
There were
Plenty of men who
Don't subscribe to
The lies this strange old world been feeding you
And honey I don't know about you
but whether they like it or not is neither here nor there
say what you want and do what you dare
But I ain't never been nobody's ugly

Till You Do Right by Me

Heard your money was getting funny
and you looking tired about the eyes
and your sleep don't come so easy
and your friendships have expired
Word is your business is no longer serious
and your charm has off and died
When you catch your own reflection are you
caught by surprise?
I mean
you had to see this coming
or maybe you thought you got off Scott-free
Well darling
when you violate MY ancestors' children
there is usually a penalty
I forgave you
but they hold grudges
they ain't quite as gracious as me
plus
God and great-GREAT-grand are best
friends
All her descendants V.I.P.
Her prayers for her lineage been like armor
in our genealogy
any weapon formed against me
will completely miss its mark
and by default
would be assailants will suffer

a consequence sweetheart
Maybe curses can be lifted
but I don't know much about those type of
things
but it looks like you are in for
an unusually cold summer
you should have never
messed
with me

Who This Woman?

I hardly recognize myself
these days
proclaiming and aspiring greatness
caring little about things
that used to matter
that should not have ever mattered
being yanked from sleep
by creativity that demands immediate
attention
willfully obliging to the best parts of myself
loving on myself
who is this woman?
undistracted by compliment or insult
welcoming the clear signs of passing time
on my face and my skin
grey is sexy
who this woman?
forgoing permission
designing her own program
evolving
getting better

I like her

A Little Shug Avery Pee

It was not entirely his fault that he felt
inadequate in the presence
of Black youth and promise
that's why they turned him loose
They too
have felt the indigestion and frustration
and incomprehension
Why,
after centuries of organized
concentrated effort
to eliminate every trace
of human strength
in a people, generation after generation
these sub-humans/super-humans
remain standing
as broad in their shoulders
as they are in their attitude?
Refusing to recognize
built in authority
not bowing
or cowering
It don't make sense
He wasn't lying when he said he was scared for his life
imagining an existence where Black boy
potential is fully realized
would be a threat to everyone's position

He was rightfully afraid
so they turned him loose
because that scared them too
He's a recognizable fellow though
sad looking - that George
weak and disturbed
measuring his man-ness on his ability to
break something
even if it has to be a child
disrupting things so as not to be mistaken
for a Nothing
Proving that murdering Potential won't make
you less of a loser
I suspect he don't eat out often
ain't no telling what's in his glass of ice
water
I know what I would give him if I ever had
the chance

Think About Heaven Later

Except for today
there has always been a tomorrow
I'm not real sure about
whether or not I will wake up in the morning
it's easy to imagine I will
seeing as I always have, since I've been born
hoping all the things I said, thought and did
will be counted as good enough
to qualify for a room in the preferred Soul Retirement Home
but I don't think about Heaven much
especially when I waved my middle finger at that truck driver
even though he deserved it
and silently judged that lady in the mall
or told that man I didn't have any change
when I had plenty because I didn't feel like stopping to dig in my purse for it
But I always bless my food
and I try to say nice things to people
and when that really annoying co-worker
does things that make me cringe
I am so patient
I hope that counts for something
I am so patient sometimes that you would know for sure that I know Jesus

I am going to think about Heaven more often
make sure I have reservations
Amen

Fine with Me

It could rain all day
the temperature could never get higher than
42 degrees
and nobody likes when it's dank and cold
but I would play outside with you and feel
warm
We could run out of gas on the freeway
in the middle of July
I would
roll up my sleeves and push that big old car
as far as I could
long as I'd be rubbing elbows with you
There could be
a meteor headed this way
imminent danger in a matter of days
and I would stay put
maybe play a hand of spades
If the last thing I'd be looking at was you, I'd
be brave
I'd eat burnt chicken and dry cake
and call it a feast
I'd clean up your sick bed like it was some
kinda treat
just an excuse to cater to you
I'd ride a camel to Indiana
I'd even drink beer
I'd go hiking and camping

let bugs dance in my hair
I'd watch an entire boxing match from
beginning to end if you going to be there
Your presence alone
puts me at ease
I believe
just about anything would be fine with me
long as I'm right next to you

I Think it Pisses God Off

What can I do to prevent my son from
catching a bullet in
the back?
 He deserves more than a final inhale of
concrete and bottom of boot
The last words he hears should be soothing
An aged wife dabbing at his brow with a
cool towel
Should be singing his favorite hymn
And telling him "it's alright, go on ahead and
see your
mama. We'll be fine here, you did good"
Instead of "f@ck your breath" by some
self appointed eliminator of further breathing
Judge jury and executioner
Ain't we all humans out here?
I would prefer not to participate in any more
candlelight vigils
I cannot press play on another recording of
murder caught on tape
10 million witnesses to injustice does not
necessarily categorize it as a crime
I've never been good at math
I guess that is why I fail to understand any
of this

My son deserves the opportunity to be big,
Black and obnoxious
He should be able to be authentic, rude and
oblivious to feelings
He should be able to reserve respect when
it is not due
He should be able to question authority
He should be able to drive too fast, and still
come home
He should not have to tuck in his shirt
Or cut his hair
Or pretend he is not as brilliant as he is to
placate folk who ain't as brilliant as he is
I am bored of this quiet rage
this aching fear
What can a mother do?
I be wondering if the Good Lord is tired of all
these
impersonators sending folk home to Glory
before they are called
That's God's job
My only solace is believing He is furious too

When the Last Time Somebody Comb Her Hair?

For the shortsighted
her knotty antennae
are a clear indication of the love she is missing
Only a child without a mama
Would be found outside of her home with her head a tangle of confusion
Prayer is intertwined with judgment as they pass
A joke about a hot-comb and 'this ain't Africa' sits in the wind
Baby girl hisses "I am Africa"
And flips her locs over her shoulder
Pities the passersby who don't know better
And steals another look at her own image smiling back at her in the store front window
Her mother encourages her to smile at herself as often as possible
Her mother loves Africa too much to burn any traces of it out her daughter's hair
What you know about a love like that?

And You Can Stay all Day

I want you to make yourself at home
here
rest yourself and be free
here
you ain't gotta go nowhere
you can stay all day
We can cuddle up
and sip black tea
while reading sappy poetry
or I could just leave you be
if you would stay all day
I've dusted corners
and the baseboards too
made these floor shine good as your
mama's do
you could eat off em if you wanted to
when you stay today
I've daydreamed of having you to myself
soak up that voice that makes me melt
the calendar couldn't move fast enough
but it is finally our day
I hope the clocks slow down
soon as you come through
there is nothing I would rather do
than share some precious time with you
I hope you will stay the day

You're a woman. You're nothing at all.

Even the Savior
was born of a woman
Your heart
learned it's cadence from a woman's
marvelous instrument
Her Body
Packaged and branded as Weaker
Was built for labor
Please don't let the softness fool you
Her Body
Contorts into comfort station or mule to fit
the need of the world
Her mind is a riddle and a masterpiece
Everything that has ever been said or done
is stored there
She will remember and remind
She can
Occupy both here and there at the same
time
at will
She recognizes the utility of tears
Washes herself in them when necessary
Baffled at how dirty some folk let
themselves get
Needlessly
A good cry is medicinal cleansing
Not the pastime of the fragile

She covers herself
If she wants to
She refuses to cover herself when she
wants to
She is policed for her wanting
Stoned for her welcoming
And ridiculed for not being ashamed
She can get the job done for cheap
She can lead and follow
She can be both invisible and distracting
She is magic
She is everything.

I Never Asked You for Anything.

"What's up sexy?"
"Smile baby."
"Where you going walking fast?"
"Let me holler for a minute."
"wit your stuck-up a$$"

Check it homie
I don't want any
I have no ear for what you are saying
I don't owe you time or attention
I do not have to smile and wave

You have
strange expectations
I've never fully understood why
I tried to care but I got tired
so it does not matter
You won't die

And I have rights
and I have my own needs
just like men folk do
consider my blank stare a sign of disinterest
you can even call me rude

cuz dude

I need to mind my business
and I need to cross the street
and I need to think of my next poem
and I need some space to think
and I need to be able to get from here to there
without flashing a ring or claiming a man

What I don't need
are reminders of what my behind is doing
I didn't wear this dress for you
If you like it that's YOUR bonus
Take a mental picture, Boo

If my resting-face is offensive
cast your eyes somewhere else
I'm not grinning all day
like some idiotic fool
so you can feel pleased with yourself

I could thank you for your compliment or
match the enthusiasm of your 'hello'
but if I don't
that is my inalienable right,
I have no debts with you.

It's Going to Rain on Your Head

You are well overdue
any minute now the winds of change
will bring you something to celebrate
you will be
drowning in favor and not debt
rejoicing with new love and increase
it will be a downpour
a cleansing shower
a joyous occasion
the drought is over
I caught a glimpse of your forecast in a dream
it is your turn to splash in the puddles
it's going to be torrential
take off your shoes
and get ready to dance in the rain

Get My Children Out of Here

This is no place to raise a child
no sane being
would lay up and bring forth
new life
in this chaotic world
all y'all crazy
cuz look at all these children
running round here innocent
smelling like dirt and looking for future
making babies involves a good time
a really good time
maybe there is a temporary loss of good
sense
during a night of good loving
or maybe y'all just like a challenge
and the scent of new baby
They curl their little hands round your finger
and you swear on everything to protect
them
you start believing you can actually keep
them safe
or you have found a patch of earth
somewhere
that hasn't been fertilized with the poison
that has been seeping into the water supply
everywhere else

turning would be humans into hateful
zombies
devoid of original thought
it ain't hardly fit for adults here
I'm bout ready for Mars

Speak Lord

I just want You to give me the answer
slide me a note with my name on it
first and last
and the word 'Answer' with an arrow
save subtle for the professionals
close and lock the door that is gateway to
Wrong Way
tighten the knob so it dare not move not
even a millimeter to the left
leave no room to suggest
I could open it if I used more force
make me weak when it is useful
snatch my pride and halt my stubborn
lighten a path at my feet
build me signs that read Yes or Stop or No
red flags have always confused me a little
I may be colorblind
gift me some foresight
awaken my wisdomignite my intuition
make me listen to myself
when I whisper genius, quiet my doubt
unriddle the puzzles
make it clear and plain
remedial would not insult me
please and thank You
Amen

I never meant to cause you any sorrow.

Baby I'm a Star

10 Million views
437,000 likes
25,000 new followers
You have their attention
For a moment or so
It was something you said or did
It was awesomely horrible or strikingly fantastic
or weird they really like weird
you could be a casualty of surveillance
or an opportunistic genius
And now, you
Person who side-stepped achievement to reach celebrity
Have been yanked out of the sea of obscurity
To have fans and enemies
Neither existed before your big moment
And they are all watching and waiting for more
Next week there will be new footage
A new voice and face ready to replace yours
You can maintain your place in cultural relevancy
By doing something else
Saying something else

Or you will
Find yourself back in the sea
Shouting status updates into crowded
murky water
Trying not to drown in ambiguity

The Beautiful Ones

Perfect penmanship
Long loops lifted in love
Signed sealed and sent
Received, relieved restored
Envelope elegant elaborate
A reminder for the recipient
"you are good enough"

Someone spent thought on her
Note is brief and powerful
The author is self-appointed family
Adopting women
Assigning them new names
Like Precious Daughter and Still Worthy
Her memory is her ministry
An anointed pen
A faithful mission
Show the girls what beauty looks like
So they can grow into women who can do the same
One's allure is not entangled in youth and bone structure
It is in the structure of one's heart
It does not age
It cannot be used up
It will outlive you

I only accept beauty-tips from women whose
Insides shine bright
Learning how to live a lovely life

Insatiable

Any response I offer to his question
No matter how thorough
Will leave room for another
 "why?"
He can watch the same episode of the same show
Two times in a row
Back-to-back
Every afternoon for a month
And request it in the morning
He will want more juice
And another ice cube
He will stall before night-night
He will recall with great detail some aspect of lazy
parenting I exhibited
And share it with random strangers in passing
"Remember we had cookies for breakfast?"
He never tires of being chased
Or jumping
Or screaming loudly for no reason
It startles me and he laughs
I love his laugh
And the fat in his thighs
And his boogie-nose
And his full body hugs
Arms tightly around my neck

And legs wrapped around my middle
Even when he is mad at me
He wants a hug from me
I'll never tire of that

Let's Go Crazy

It's not that there is nothing we can do
It's that there is nothing we are willing to do
We could change the course of things if we wanted to
Hands would have to get dirty
Backs would be broken
Persons would turn up missing
But
That is what is happening anyway
For free
It should cost somebody something
Doing away with a perfectly good human being...
It should be too expensive
A heavy price might be a deterrent
Might change things if they just couldn't afford to make those types of decisions
The winds would surely shift
Then we could go back to doing whatever it is we did before we were worthless
When we were all divine

We could do something

Take Me with You

I want to come
Grant me access
Bring me backwards
Show me your monsters
I'll show you mine
We'll cower together
Lend me your courage
Brave us a future
Where we can love proper
Open journals
Peel off bandage
Expose old wound
Prevent new injury
Reveal hiding places
Wipe off the makeup
Give me your ugly
I'll keep your secrets
They'll help me navigate
Copilot the next leg
And the last leg
Let's ride

Adore

Messed around and got me writing about you
you keep it up
and I will be spilling my guts
in iambic pentameter
and haiku
stop playin
for I have me an entire chapbook titled "You"
and then they will start to call me obsessed
and crazy
but there ain't really an artist worth naming
that has never been called Crazy
call me crazy if you want to
as long as you keep calling
there is epic sonnet in this thing right here
too much free verse in our last conversation
overflow of Ballade in your embrace
we are a limerick when nobody is watching
but you are a poem
all by yourself

The Glamourous Life

They stare
laid hair
face beat
brows fleek
waist snatched
breasts fake
a$$ real
hips wide
thighs thick
feet perched
five inch
name brand
paid fly
wants gets
loves last
works hard
gym sweat
job flex
all day
for her
own self
keep up
who with?
please bish
watch this

Round and Round

It surprised her
the first time
a sprained wrist
was easy to explain away
he was ashamed
she packed her things
and stayed with her sister
he plead and promised
they prayed and cried
she returned
her sister cussed
and threatened
they forgave

the second time
she was embarrassed
could not tell her sister
she did not pretend to leave
the bruise around her eye was
trashy
he went somewhere for a little while
he came back
he plead and promised
they prayed and cried
she stayed

the last time

he loosened her tooth
her Daddy worked an extra job
to pay for those straight white teeth
she died a little
he looked at her
like she was pathetic
she found some pride
in box of old photos and awards in the attic
she used to be bound for great things
she found some crazy at the bottom of a bottle
of vodka
he woke up on fire
she called her sister
they prayed and cried
and laughed
"bout time bitch"

Kiss

Public affection
has a bad reputation
why should we wait until nobody is looking
to remind each other we are connected
Way I figure
the world could use a little more public
loving
There is something joyous about noses
brushing
and cheeks flushing
and hands reaching to pull a body closer
ain't nothing indecent about lips meeting
and tugging on one another
pressing and searching and exchanging…
it's sweet
I even read somewhere it burns calories
Sugar is good for you
go get you some
there is plenty

Still Waiting

I'll be the one
wearing
nothing
but a pair of Fulani earrings
and everything I have ever dared to care
about will be
weaved into the fabric covering my arms
keeping me warm and making me cold
my knees will be bruised from desperate
prayers with your name in them
I will be the one singing your praises
it will be me
You should know
I still wait for you
while I work
while I plan
while I dream I am waiting
while I play
while I fight your wars
and mine
I still wait
for the relief that is your belief in me
for the compliment in your approval
for you to knead the tension from my back
and my shoulders
for you to need what I have
for you to want what I have

You should know
that I have been waiting
for you
to recognize
me

A Love Bizarre

I don't know where his lips have been, but it doesn't matter
I know where they are now
I don't know how anyone could spew his name like it is some vile slur
It makes the corners of my mouth tilt upwards every single time I say it
I don't care about the Used-to-Loves
Except for
Whomever it was
Who set him free
so he could be here
lovin on me
He should thank her…
In an imaginary letter
that he never writes
or even thinks about too hard
Forget it
Let's pretend
It's only ever been us
And that's all it ever needs to be

Sexy Mutha@#$%!*
(a haiku)

He said I do not
have to be able to cook
to take care of him.

One Song

Nobody saying two arms ain't better than
one
All I'm saying is
if all you got is one arm
then that one arm will have to do
you can return all pity to sender
or feel sorry for yourself on occasion
but we won't allow that to be some recurring
excuse to avoid excellence
the other arm didn't have enough muscle
power and dexterity to hold you up
every arm ain't fit with a helping hand on the
end
and that may have been a distraction
but we will never know
it is not your fault
these are the cards you were dealt
but you should know, you can still win
you got one good arm
one really good, prayed up arm
one arm can solidify an agreement
can open doors
wipe a tear
hug you close
point you in the right direction
you can praise God with one arm
this ain't going to be some tragic statistic

write your victory speech now
with your one arm having self
you will be better than fine
you'll be great

If I Was Your Girlfriend

I saw her up close one time
measured her beauty against mine
and didn't come up short.
I didn't get it.
Heard she handles her business like a boss
but I been doing that forever
Rumor is she can't cook
My macaroni and cheese is famous in at
least three counties
My feet are smaller
My family is bigger
My booty sits higher
My kisses are tender
I read my Bible
Give to the needy
Love on the children
and volunteer with the elderly
If this were a contest
and he was the prize
Then he should be sitting over here
staring into MY eyes
When I finally broke down and asked him
why
in between tears of frustration and rejection
and pride
he responded with a smile about a mile
wide

"She's not a better woman than you.
But she is the perfect woman for me."
which didn't make any sense until I saw
them together
and she was laughing wildly at one of his
dry jokes
she thinks he's funny
he better hold on to her

Acknowledgments

This is Lynnette's third collection of poetry. *Purple* is preceded by *I've Been Meaning to Tell You* released February 2014 and *Only Love Can do That,* October 2015. The inspiration for this project began in April of the same year, as part of a poem-a-day writing challenge. The theme is a recommendation from a friend through social media. Lynnette shared "*Sista, You been on my Mind",* the first poem in the book, on her Facebook page. She chose a few more, famous lines from the film, **The Color Purple**, to serve as writing prompts for other poems. Joy Ward suggested a book titled *Purple*. It would include all the pieces that were shared. That was the beginning. This was an easy birth compared to Lynnette's previous babies. She would like to thank the artists who laid down the ground work. Tremendous gratitude to Alice Walker, for her brilliant novel turned classic film and the actors who brought her words to life. She would also like to thank Prince, also known as The Purple One, for spinning words into rhythm and magic, and being responsible for hit songs many are not aware he wrote. Purple is more than everyone's favorite color. It is an experience.

Made in the USA
Middletown, DE
12 April 2016